Veterinarian

Workers YOU Know

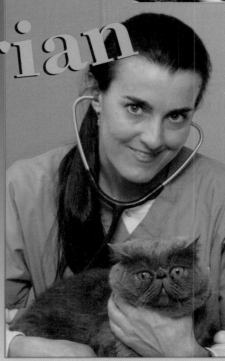

Veterinarian

Kathleen Ermitage

RAINTREE
STECK-VAUGHN
PUBLISHERS

RSVP

A Harcourt Company

Austin   New York
www.steck-vaughn.com

Published by Raintree Steck-Vaughn Publishers,
an imprint of Steck-Vaughn Company

Art Director: Max Brinkmann
Editor: Pam Wells
Design and Illustration: Proof Positive/Farrowlyne Associates, Inc.
Planned and Produced by
Proof Positive/Farrowlyne Associates, Inc.

Library of Congress Cataloging-in-Publication Data
Ermitage, Kathleen.
    Veterinarian/Kathleen Ermitage.
      p. cm. — (Workers you know)
    Summary: A small animal veterinarian tells about her job as well as about that of zoo and farm animal doctors.
      ISBN 0–8172–5592–3
      1. Veterinarians—Juvenile literature. 2. Veterinary medicine—Vocational guidance—Juvenile literature. [1. Veterinarians. 2. Veterinary medicine—Vocational guidance. 3. Vocational guidance.] I. Title. II. Series.

SF756 .E74 2000
636.089′023—dc21
                                                                                         99–054427

Printed and bound in the United States
1 2 3 4 5 6 7 8 9 0 LB 03 02 01 00

Acknowledgments:
Photo Credits: **7:** © K. D. Lawson/stockphoto.com; **14:** © Eric and David Hosking/Corbis; **26:** © Kathi Lamm/Tony Stone Images; **29:** © David de Lossy, Ghislain & Marie/The Image Bank

Note: You will find more information about becoming a veterinarian on the last page of this book.

Can you tell why Laura is smiling? She is smiling because she just picked out the puppy she wants to adopt. If you love animals as much as Laura does, you may want to think about working with animals when you grow up. You can work with cows on a dairy farm. You can write books and articles about animals. You can even travel around the world photographing wild animals, like polar bears and water buffalo, from a safe distance. Or, you can help animals stay healthy by becoming a veterinarian, like me.

Hi. My name is Kim Wilson, and I'm a doctor for animals. This kind of a doctor is a veterinarian. When animals get sick or are hurt, it is my job to figure out what's wrong and take care of them. I also help owners learn how to take care of their pets, so the animals will stay healthy.

After Laura adopted her puppy, she brought it to my office. She wanted to make sure her puppy was healthy.

My office is at an animal hospital. We have special equipment at the animal hospital, just like doctors have for human patients at regular hospitals. We have ultrasound machines and X-ray equipment to help us identify medical problems. We can even do surgery here!

But I won't be doing any surgery today. Laura's puppy is here for a routine checkup. A checkup is an examination to make sure a person or an animal is healthy.

Do you see my stethoscope? Your doctor probably has one, too. I use my stethoscope to listen to the puppy's heartbeat. I also check its breathing. I use a thermometer to take the puppy's temperature. Dogs normally have a temperature between 101 and 102 degrees. A human's temperature is usually 98.6 degrees.

Next, I look at the puppy's eyes, ears, nose, and mouth. I use special equipment to help me see better. First, I check for pinkness inside the puppy's eyelids. I also make sure that the puppy's gums and tongue are nice and pink. The pink color tells me the puppy is healthy. Then I check the puppy's teeth. A veterinarian is not only a dog's doctor, but also its dentist!

I also check the puppy for fleas. Fleas are tiny bugs that live on pets and make them itch. If animals could talk, they would tell you that fleas are no fun!

Joel helps me give the checkup. Joel is a new veterinarian. He just finished veterinary school. Veterinarians have to go to school for seven years—that's about 4,000 hours of classes! They have to learn thousands of medical words and their meanings. They have to know how to pronounce all of them, too!

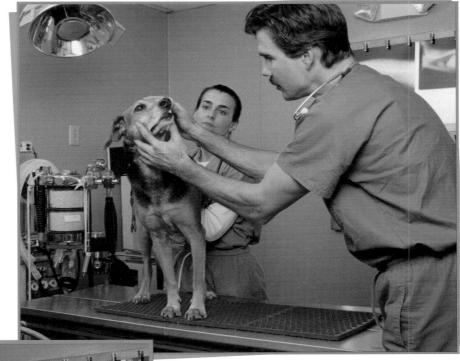

Now Joel is practicing the things he learned in school. Joel and I do not find anything wrong during the checkup. This is one healthy puppy!

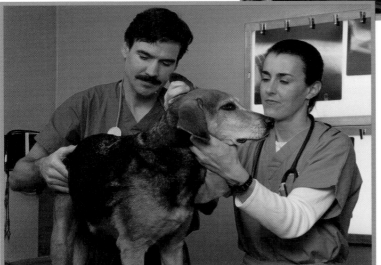

9

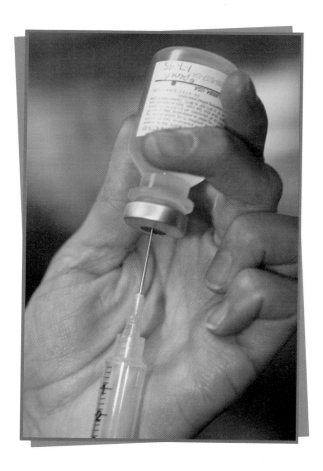

After the checkup, I give the puppy a shot. The shot is called a vaccination (vack-suh-**nay**-shun). Vaccinations keep people and animals from getting certain diseases. Have you ever gotten a vaccination? It stings a little, but it keeps you healthy.

Vaccinating pets helps to keep people healthy, too. People can catch some diseases that animals get. For example, a person who is bitten by an animal with rabies can also get rabies.

This is Rory, the receptionist for the animal hospital. I write down the vaccinations that I gave Laura's puppy. Rory will put this information in the computer. It's important for Rory to check her work. This way she will make sure she puts the correct information into the computer. A year from now, Rory will print out a card and send it to Laura. The card will remind Laura that it is time for her puppy's checkup.

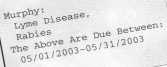

Kim's Animal Hospital

Annual vaccinations are an important part of your pet's health. Our records show that your pet is now due. Please call us today to make an appointment.

Murphy:
Lyme Disease,
Rabies
The Above Are Due Between:
05/01/2003-05/31/2003

Once I am done with the puppy, I talk with Laura. Teaching pet owners to take good care of their pets is part of my job. I explain everything carefully, but I will also give Laura a list of instructions in case she forgets.

Pets depend on their owners for everything. Dogs need to be fed and given water every day. They need to be walked and played with every day. They also need to be bathed when they get dirty.

Veterinarians take care of some unusual pets. They have to understand what weather conditions are like in different parts of the world. John's pet is an iguana. In the wild, iguanas live in warm, tropical climates. Iguanas cannot go outside when it is very cold.

Today, it is very cold outside. John cannot bring his iguana to my office, so I go to his home to give the iguana a checkup.

Whenever I visit John's iguana, I wonder how I look to it. Iguanas have eyes on both sides of their heads, so they can see two different pictures at once. This is something like what you would see if you had eyes on the back of your head as well as the front. In the wild, iguanas use their vision to help them jump from tree branch to tree branch.

Squeegee is an African gray parrot. Her new owner, Tammara, asked me to stop by and check Squeegee's home—her cage. First, I make sure the cage is big enough for Squeegee. I make sure there is room for Squeegee to open both wings and move around. I also make sure the

cage is not made out of any type of metal that could poison Squeegee, because parrots sometimes chew on their cages.

Squeegee's cage looks nice and clean, and I tell Tammara how important it is to keep it that way. Parrots can get sick if their cages are not cleaned regularly.

Then I talk to Squeegee herself! An African gray parrot is said to be about as smart as a five-year-old child. Squeegee can say more than 100 different words. She can also mimic the sound of the phone ringing and repeat Tammara's answering machine message!

Tammara told me that Squeegee's parents were somebody's pets, too. I'm glad. In the wild, parrots live in parts of South America, Africa, and Australia. Parrots that are captured in the wild often do not survive the trip to the United States.

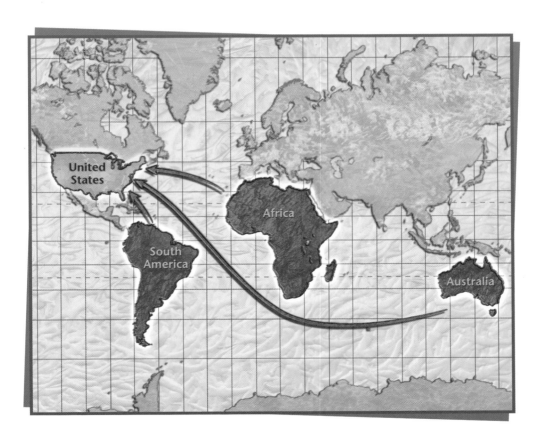

Parrots and iguanas aren't the only unusual pets I see. Meet Hugo, a red-tail boa constrictor. Snakes can get sick and catch colds, just like you and I can. But it's hard to tell when a snake is sick—that's where I come in.

What can you do if your pet snake catches a cold? Loss of appetite or a change in the way the snake usually moves are the two best signs that a snake is sick. When snakes get sick, they need basically the same things you do—warmth and plenty of rest. Sometimes, snake owners have to give their pets water through a tube. At the animal hospital, if a snake needs water very badly, we sometimes inject the water under the snake's skin.

I take care of lots of different kinds of pets. So far you've seen a dog, an iguana, a parrot, and a snake. Can you think of anything all these animals

have in common? They are all small animals. I'm a small animal veterinarian. I also take care of some other small animals—like cats, hamsters, and rabbits. But some veterinarians take care of large animals—very large animals.

My friend Dale is a veterinarian in a zoo. He is the doctor for all the animals there. It can be an elephant-sized job! The animals in a zoo have to be cared for twenty-four hours a day.

Dale

Part of Dale's job is to make sure that baby animals, like baby elephants, are growing fast enough. Dale weighs the baby animals and makes a chart showing how fast they are growing. His graphs look like the ones you might see in a math or a science class when you are older.

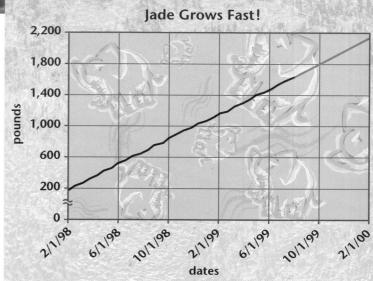

Jade Grows Fast!

pounds

dates

Just like me, Dale has to be both a doctor and a dentist for the animals he cares for. Animal teeth are different from your teeth. Sometimes a llama's teeth may grow too long. That can be bad for the llama because the llama will have trouble chewing its food. If this happens, Dale files down the llama's teeth, so that they are shorter.

Three or four times a year, Dale has to trim each llama's claws. It's not an easy job, because llamas do not like to have their legs touched. Dale goes slowly and talks to the llamas gently as he works. Often he brings them treats to sweeten their tempers!

Veterinarian

Sometimes, lions and other animals are moved from one zoo to another. Before that can happen, Dale examines the animals to make sure they are healthy. He makes sure their vaccinations are up to date. Then, he types up a set of papers that show it is safe for the animals to travel.

The parts of a veterinarian's job that seem routine to me can be challenging for Dale. How do you take the temperature of a full-grown lion? Very carefully! A lion weighs more than three hundred pounds. It needs medicine to keep it calm so it won't hurt Dale while he takes its temperature.

Maria

This is Maria. She's one of the zookeepers. Just like house cats, lions need to be fed and given water every day. But there are some differences. First of all, lions eat a lot more than house cats do. They each can eat seventy-five pounds of food in a single meal!

Keeping the animals clean in a zoo is important. If the animals and their cages are not clean, the animals can get sick. Sometimes Maria even helps to give baths to some animals.

Bob

Have you ever been to a farm? My friend Bob is a farm veterinarian. He is a doctor for horses, cattle, pigs, and sheep. A horse can cut its leg on a fence. Then, it's important for Bob to wash the wound and put a bandage on the leg. This treatment will help the cut heal faster.

Like other farm veterinarians, Bob works with the farmers or ranchers to make sure their livestock are healthy. He gives checkups, performs surgery, and gives vaccinations.

He tests the animals' food to make sure it is nutritious (new-**trish**-us). He even delivers babies. Every time Bob sees a newborn calf stand up, he feels good.

Veterinarian

Keeping cows healthy is important because people drink the milk that comes from cows. Bob will test the cows' milk to make sure it is safe. He uses a microscope like the ones you might have seen in your science class. Bob will make sure the cows' milk is not carrying any diseases. He will also check to make sure nothing has gotten into the cows' milk.

Suddenly my pager starts beeping. Remember Rory, the receptionist at my office? She calls my pager when there is an emergency. When the pager beeps, I know someone needs my help. Just like doctors, veterinarians have to be ready to drop what they're doing if an animal is hurt. I hurry back to my office.

Wayne

Back at my office, Wayne is checking a dog that is having trouble walking. My guess is that the dog has a sprained or broken leg.

I am a little worried that this dog might be in shock. A person or an animal can go into shock when something upsetting or painful happens. Shock can make it harder for an animal to stay warm and to heal. To check for shock, I check the dog's heartbeat on the inside of its leg. Then, I take its temperature.

I have an idea about what is wrong with this dog, but I need to be sure. John, my X-ray technician, uses a special camera to take a radiograph of the dog's leg. A radiograph (**ray**-dee-oh-graf) is a picture produced by X rays. X rays cause bones and organs under your skin to give off light so they can be seen in a photograph.

A radiograph is just one of the special tools that we use here at the animal hospital. We also use microscopes like the one you saw Bob using. Sometimes, though, we send things out to a laboratory to be tested. For example, if this dog was sick, we might do a blood test and send the blood to a laboratory. The laboratory could look at the blood and tell us if the dog had an infection.

John

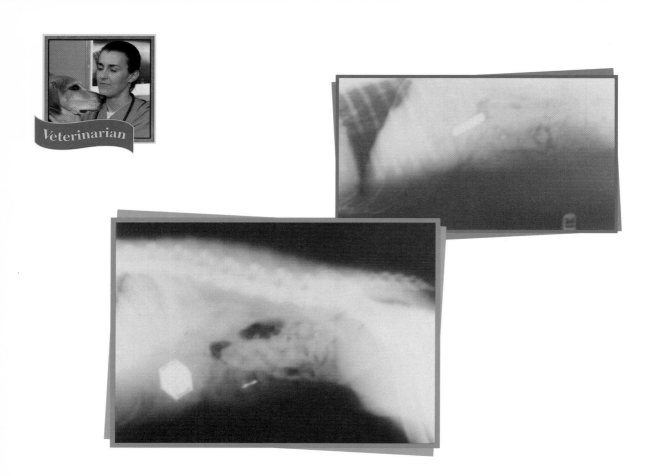

    This is the radiograph of the dog's leg. I was right. One of the dog's hind legs is broken. An animal's hind legs are its back legs. Do you see where the leg is broken?

    As soon as a bone breaks, the body starts to fix it. The bones begin growing back together. But the bones must be kept in the correct position and protected while they grow back. That is where veterinarians can help.

We protect bones by putting them in casts. A cast is a stiff wrap that goes around an injured limb. I put a cast on the dog's leg. In about a month, the bones should be healed and strong again. Then, I will take the cast off.

This is another X-ray technician and his assistant. Their animal hospital is in a different city. They also need to use X rays to be sure that a bone is broken.

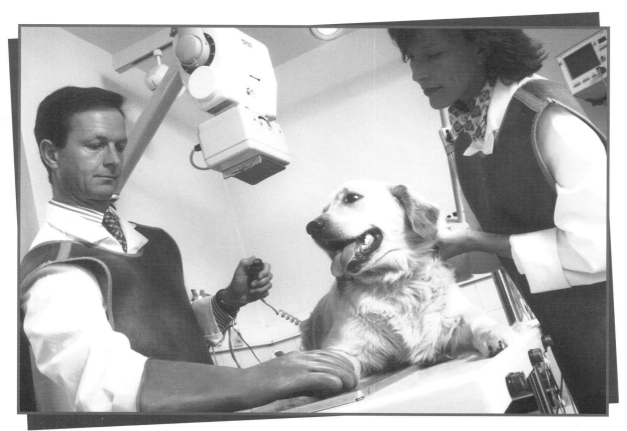

After I get home, I take my
dog out for a walk. And guess
who I see? Laura and her puppy.
They look very happy together.

Veterinarian

People and animals can be best friends. That is why I am a veterinarian. I make sure our animal friends stay healthy.

For Information About Becoming a Veterinarian, Contact:
The American Veterinary Medical Association
1931 North Meacham Road, Suite 100
Schaumburg, IL 60173-4360

For Information About Veterinary Science Programs for Children, Contact:
National 4-H Council
7100 Connecticut Avenue
Chevy Chase, MD 20815-4999

Veterinarian Education, Training, and Requirements:
Veterinarians must complete seven years of college training through an approved veterinary program to become a Doctor of Veterinary Medicine (DVM). They must also pass at least one certification test at both the state and the national level. Many states also require veterinarians to attend continuing education courses to maintain their licenses.

Related Careers:

Veterinary Technician	Veterinary Surgeon
Health Inspector	Zoo Dietitian
Agricultural Scientist	Pet Groomer